Reality Of Realty

Dr. Adv. HARSHUL SAVLA
V.P. Lobo

INDIA • SINGAPORE • MALAYSIA

Notion Press

No.8, 3rd Cross Street,
CIT Colony, Mylapore,
Chennai, Tamil Nadu – 600004

First Published by Notion Press 2021
Copyright © Dr. Adv. Harshul Savla, V.P. Lobo 2021
All Rights Reserved.

ISBN 978-1-63806-543-2

This book has been published with all efforts taken to make the material error-free after the consent of the author. However, the author and the publisher do not assume and hereby disclaim any liability to any party for any loss, damage, or disruption caused by errors or omissions, whether such errors or omissions result from negligence, accident, or any other cause.

While every effort has been made to avoid any mistake or omission, this publication is being sold on the condition and understanding that neither the author nor the publishers or printers would be liable in any manner to any person by reason of any mistake or omission in this publication or for any action taken or omitted to be taken or advice rendered or accepted on the basis of this work. For any defect in printing or binding the publishers will be liable only to replace the defective copy by another copy of this work then available.

ABOUT THE AUTHOR

Dr. Adv. Harshul Savla (MRICS)

Dr. Adv. Harshul Savla (MRICS) is Principal Partner of M Realty (Suvidha Lifespaces) which has successfully completed more than 1.2 million sq.ft. in last 30 years across Mumbai City under the able leadership of Mr. Pramesh Rambhiya. CRISIL India recognized Dr. Harshul as "Young Thought Leader" and Realty NXT featured him as "Young Turk of Real Estate Sector". He has won the prestigious CREDAI-MCHI Golden Pillar Award in the category of Best Debutant Real Estate Developer and has been awarded "Young Achiever of the Year" by ET NOW, CNN News 18, ZEE Business, MAHARASHTRA Times, ABP News, MID DAY and Realty Quarter.

Dr. Harshul has worked as EA to Ramesh Nair, CEO and Country Head at JLL, India and has worked in the Wealth Management Team at TATA Capital. He is a perfect blend of Corporate Experience along with stellar education credentials of Ph.D., LL.M, LL.B, MBA and BMS. Apart from this he is an NSE Certified Market Professional -

About the Author

Level 4 and has done a course on 'Strategic Real Estate Management' from ISB, Hyderabad. As a matter of fact, he is one of the youngest Office Bearer in the Managing Committee of CREDAI-MCHI wherein he is the Convener of Research & Analytics Wing and looks into the Learning and Development Initiatives.

Dr. Harshul is also an Amazon Best Selling Author and has authored one of India's most comprehensive books on Real Estate Sector. Some of his books are: ERA Post RERA, Real Estate Laws, Reality of Realty, Real Estate Valuation, Affordable Housing, NBFC & HFC Crisis, Fractional Ownership & REITs, Insolvency & Bankruptcy Code, Self-Redevelopment & Reviving Stalled Projects, Luxury Retail and COVID-O-NOMICS. He regularly writes articles for fortnightly business magazine Property House.

Dr. Harshul is also a Visiting Faculty at the prestigious RICS School of Built Environment, Mumbai Campus. Harshul teaches the subject 'Real Estate Development Process' to Management Students at the Mumbai Campus. He is also Guest Lecturer at REMI - The Real Estate Management Institute, Mumbai. He was Invited to conduct Session on REITs in India for Developers Members of NAREDCO and was one of the youngest Member Developer to do so. He has also delivered a lecture at PEATA (I) on Future of Realty.

About the Author

V.P. Lobo

V.P. Lobo is Post Graduate in Business Management with 23 years of Real Estate industry experience. He has held various senior management positions in large construction companies such as CEO of Rustomjee-Evershine joint venture company, Director- Operations of Agarwal Group, Vice President of Marg Limited. Presently, he is the Chairman & Managing Director of T3 Urban Developers Ltd. and Managing Partner of Reboot Realty.

He has been known in the industry circles for his exceptional marketing skills. He is known to have built and sold projects in toughest markets. He is also known as one of the biggest blogger in the industry and his blogs have been read by the industry big wigs as well as the authorities in the government. Besides being a visiting faculty management and engineering colleges, he has been contributing to the industry by training tomorrow's professionals.

In this book, his popular blogs have been reproduced in which he has brought out the nuances of real estate business in simple language to enable the common man to understand the intricacies of the industry.

The proceeds of this book will go to his charity trust T3 Hope Foundation which helps the poor rural children get quality English Medium education to enable them to compete with the city children.

CONTENTS

1. Real Estate ही Real है। — 9
2. The Reality of Realty — 15
3. Real Estate's Revival Is Economy's Survival — 22
4. Property Price Crash – a Mirage! — 29
5. Perils of Price Cut — 33
6. (Un)Affordable Housing! — 37
7. Reboot Realty — 41
8. Fortune Favours the Brave — 45
9. Market Is Good If Marketing Is Good — 49
10. All Is Well When You Sell — 53
11. Lenders Could Make 'Housing for All' Possible — 55
12. Science of Home Buying — 62
13. Post COVID, Developer's Profits Are in the Kitchen — 66
14. Is Realty Strong Enough for COVID-19 — 70
15. New Normal: Real Estate Strategies Post Lockdown — 73

Strategies to Be Adopted by Developers Post Lockdown — 77

CHAPTER 1
REAL ESTATE ही REAL है।

EVOLUTION

The history of Real Estate has evolved simultaneously with the evolution of humankind. From the Cave Man to the modern suited booted, not so Gentle Man, the Real Estate has kept pace through the wheel of revolution. In fact, the man has always been known by the Real Estate he occupied, either as a noun or as an adjective. The Cave Man earned his food by hunting till he moved to agriculture as his daily bread. Scientific proof tells us that this shift took place around 30,000 B.C and this transition also heralded the advent of the most original form of investment - Real Estate Ownership.

SCRIPTURES

The Holy Bible, Old and New Testament, has 22 references to Real Estate transactions. Two of the Ten Commandments uphold the sanctity of owning property. "Thou Shall Not Steal" and "Thou Shall Not Covet" explicitly indicate private property ownership. The Ten Commandments are supposed to have been given to Moses around 20,000 B.C.

We find a reference to Real Estate in The Holy Quran, where the WILL is mandated to inherit property. In fact, The Holy Quran has extensive chapters outlining the laws of inheritance. The present-day requirement of witnesses while registering the property, is indeed mentioned in The Holy Quran.

The Upanishads, Vedas and various other Holy Scriptures have innumerable references to the transition from the common use of land to private ownership of Real Estate. Most importantly, these Holy Scriptures highlight the divine significance of Real Estate by recognizing it as sacred. It is strongly believed that bloodshed of innocent and violence over a piece of Real Estate carries the burden of sin.

The historical, spiritual, religious, and economic heritage of Real Estate proves that it is undoubtedly the oldest and most original investment avenue in humankind's history.

AURA

The aura of Real Estate continues to dominate the Anno Domini (AD) era as well. What could not be purchased was invaded as a result of great wars. The more the potential of the Real Estate, the greater was the war. Every Kingdom had the ultimate desire of owning maximum Real Estate.

East India Company was essentially a Real Estate company owning lands in India including Mumbai. And when you own Real Estate, the offshoots are plenty, generating additional regular income besides capital appreciation. Large swathes of Tea & Coffee estates in the hills were testimonials for Britishers' astute Real Estate sense. Be it our Parliament House or President's Palace, Britishers were great Real Estate creators and investors.

KINGDOMS

The Kings and Queens of India were equally shrewd in Real Estate development. Even after hundreds of years, we continue to admire the monuments they created, which stand as a glowing tribute to their interest in Real Estate.

TODAY'S BILLIONAIRES

Finally, we come to the contemporary world. The easiest way to explain Real Estate and how it holds sway over the modern world economy would be to mention the number of billionaires in the world who owe their billions to Real Estate. Almost 40% of the world's billionaires are from the Real Estate Industry. This speaks volumes for the Real Estate and its sheer capacity to create wealth.

ECONOMY

In my blog titled, "Real Estate's Revival is Economy's Survival", I have dwelt on the undeniable role of Real Estate in Economy. Be it Seven Wonders Of The World or Tallest Building In The World, be it Disney World or World's Largest Palace Complex, everything is Real Estate.

Real estate still holds the same position, importance, and significance through humankind's evolution and revolution over many thousands of years. Though the definition, meaning, grandeur, size and shape of Real Estate has gone through massive changes, it has survived through the greatest of great wars. It has prospered in worst recessions the world has gone through. It has thrived among plagues and famines. Have no doubt it will endure the onslaught of COVID-19 too. After all, it is the first and most original investment man has ever made, and it has stood the test of time. The nature of Real Estate is such that it is available to enjoy now and for the generations to come. Investment in Real Estate is the most sensible decision man has ever made in the history of humankind.

Love it. Hate it. But you can't ignore it. Because in a surreal world, "Real Estate ही Real है!"

Gold Price at Rs. 50,000 per 10gms is at an all-time high!

Stock Markets Volatility is at an all-time high!

Mutual Funds Stability is at an all-time low!

Bank FDs now fetch less than Savings Accounts!

10 REASONS WHY *"FD TODO READY FLAT KHAREEDO!"* MAKE SENSE

1. Residential offers fixed returns of FD and capital appreciation of stocks with stability

2. Prices of Real Estate have not increased in the last five years, despite the rising Costs!

   - NBFC Crisis (ILFS & DHFL) – liquidity crunch, new sanctions affected
   - Banks not passing the benefit of RBI REPO rate Cuts – interest cost has increased
   - No reduction in Circle Rates / Ready Reckoner Rates – Increased BMC Premium Rates
   - Cartelization by ancillary industries like cement, steel etc. have increased the cost of the product
   - GST on the under-construction property – demotivates buyer to purchase under-construction properties
   - Lockdown has resulted in Increased labour cost, loss of interest, loss of overheads. Thus, it will be safe to assume that Real Estate is today at its lowest possible valuation

3. Strong capital appreciation is possible within the next 5 Years for projects which are Ready to Move in today given that no price rise has occurred despite an increase in costs

4. Negligible new launches in the next two years. Hence, supply would be curtailed in the short term

5. Ready fats have ZERO project execution risk!

6. ZERO GST! on ready flats

7. Often re-sale flats in old buildings have structural & leakage issues

8. New projects offer better planning which has almost zero wastage

9. Strong leasing demand – while your FD / saving accounts is only offering you interest that too meagre, real estate will provide you with regular income and capital appreciation in near future

10. Realty is a wealth protector; stocks could drive you towards bankruptcy too

Those living in rental homes have realized the importance of being in their own homes while NRIs facing challenging times in their present domiciles are looking at creating a safe haven 'back home' in India. Demand for additional space for home offices is on the rise, with the need for more efficient layouts. The importance of standard amenities, business centres and more open spaces will be an inherent part of the new demand criteria in the post-COVID-19 world. It clearly shows that potential homebuyers searching for flats have pressed a pause button for the time being because of liquidity concerns and uncertainty over the COVID pandemic. But, a majority of them will gradually start returning to the market in the coming months.

Real estate has always been less volatile than share markets, making it the safest investment available. The preference of this new age home buyer has also changed due to the crisis, and it is imperative for us to adapt to new technologies that will ease the entire home buying process.

"Real Estate is Real Investment. Buy a Home & Secure your Family's Future NOW!"

CHAPTER 2

THE REALITY OF REALTY

The image that comes to a layman's mind when he hears the words 'Real Estate Developer' is a multi-millionaire, pot-bellied, half bald, gold-laden, corrupt, opportunistic, greedy entrepreneur, who makes his wealth through profiteering, scams and frauds! Unfortunately, media has a massive contribution in building that image perception of a Real Estate Developer. Let me put forth a few questions before you which have been conveniently never highlighted.

Q1. Which is the only business where one sows the seeds today and gets the results only after 4 to 10 years?

REAL ESTATE. Because the developer decides on day one and faces all vagaries and uncertainties, right from the land title to government policies, market fluctuations and ever-changing customer preferences. A Real Estate Developer complies with more than 80 Acts and obtains more than 100 NOC's to deliver a product!

Q2. Which is the only business where the so-called sharks, that is, the moneylenders, try to grab the maximum share of profit irrespective of the uncertainty of profit or loss?

REAL ESTATE. It is the sole business that pays maximum interest to money lenders, whether NBFC or HFC or private lenders. In other activities like farming, the government supports the farmers and also regulates money lenders. In the case of farmers, the government does not hesitate in writing off the principal debt of farmers, but for developers, it slaps penalties and prosecutions. All types of industries get some relief from financers such as priority sector lending and such provisions, but there is never any priority or relief for real estate. The same bank which lends to NBFC at 10% and the NBFC lends to the developer at 18%. Why can't the bank directly not lend to the developer?? Why can't we have a Real Estate Bank (on the lines of NABARD, SIDBI etc.)

Q3. Which is the business which generates maximum livelihood for people?

REAL ESTATE. Real estate is the second largest employer in India. Today employment creation is the fundamental challenge for our economy. One would invest 100 billion rupees and generate employment for 1000 to 10000 people. Real estate creates far more employment compared to the investment involved. This sector is the highest to offer livelihood to migrant workers. It has provided survival and allowed a better lifestyle and more aspiration even to the economically challenged segment of the population. A Real Estate Developer works with more than 250 Ancillary Industries and with more than five crore Labors across India to deliver realty.

Q4. Which business attracts maximum negative attention from politicians?

REAL ESTATE. It is always at the mercy of politicians and bureaucrats. The land is the primary raw material for real estate, and that is under the control of the government and indirectly, the politicians. Developers always find themselves at the mercy of these two power wielders. Policies are still framed in the government's interest that earns maximum revenue in the form of a cess, premiums, income tax, GST, labour cess etc. A developer has to obtain 100+ individual NOCs even today, which contributes to project delays, why can't we have a Single Window Approvals System ??

Q5. Who is the major contributor to the GDP?

REAL ESTATE. It contributes 7 percent of India's GDP. Globally it is proven that real estate helps nations to pull their economies out of recession. China is the classic example to demonstrate this; in 2008-09, after the Lehman-Global Financial Crisis, China concentrated on its real estate development. It was the first country to pull out of recession with GDP growth as high as 7-8 percent. The Demographic Dividend of India in terms of Young Population will soon turn from Boon to Bane if they are not productively engaged and employed.

Q6. Which is the business which suffers maximum due to cartelization?

REAL ESTATE. The business suffers maximum due to cartelization at the hands of related industries. Cement manufacturers are one such example where prices have been increased unscrupulously. Cement manufacturers have been levied huge penalties by Competition Commission of India even in the past due to their restrictive trade practices. They challenged them in the Supreme Court and managed to get a stay order. Yet, the cement industry continues with its uncouth policies, creates cartels and hikes up prices. So far, the government has turned a blind eye to cement industry's wrongdoings and not taken any firm policies against the monopolistic price rise. The judiciary has also not taken any steps against this exploitative situation by the cement manufacturers.

Q7. What business can salvage the overall economy from the after-effects of COVID?

REAL ESTATE. It has been proved that almost 250 industries are dependent on real estate. Today two steel industry giants have been downgraded by rating agencies. All ancillary industries can come out of recession as real estate can generate demand for these industries. The government can only focus on Real Estate and Infrastructure, which can get the wheel of an economy running.

Q8. Which industry has suffered maximum by directives that force it to sell its products at no profit- no loss or complete loss policy?

Yes, this is unbelievable but true. Real estate is the only industry that has been at the receiving end of the most ruthless attitude from the bureaucracy, prominent bankers and politicians. Their only advice is to clear the real estate stock irrespective of the price at which it sells as if its perishable vegetables grown in a few months and have a shelf life of hardly few days.

Silence of the Lambs - Suffering Of Real Estate, a COVID Reflection.

Award-winning Hollywood movie, 'Silence of the Lambs', is fresh in my mind and the mute suffering of Judie Foster's character, made me adopt the name of the movie as part of the title of my blog.

'If you can't be anything, you can be a developer', was the common refrain in the pre-IT revolution era. And it wasn't entirely incorrect. The economic liberalization which began in 1991 (coincidentally, the year in which Silence Of the Lamb was released), introduced a different breed of developers to the industry. The entry of dynamic individuals with aggressive plans to change the skyline in an unregulated atmosphere was the industry's turning point. The traditional approach gave way for modern methods of doing business. Easy access to the banking sector, enhanced development opportunities, entry of professionals etc., gave wings to these dream merchants' dreams. The business flourished and became a significant contributor to the economy. No wonder, the real estate industry continues to support more than 275 ancillary industries single-handedly. It also happens to be the second-largest employment generator in the country.

Well, as they say, 'every day is not a Sunday'. We all know that real estate business is cyclical. However, the present situation has gone beyond the industry's cyclical nature, inflicting suffering and pain on the developers, most of which was due to circumstances beyond developers' reach. The industry has been silently suffering, like a sacrificial lamb.

EXTORTIONATE FEES

As the construction activities picked up, the authorities found methods to impose approval windows with varieties of levies, charges, fees and penalties, using every possible excuse at every stage of construction. More often than not, this became the deciding factor for the success or failure of the project. Worst, this aspect is so complicated that it is beyond the understanding of common man. The developer has no voice and no choice in this matter at all.

COSTS

A real estate is virtually an assembling unit than a production factory. It is created by assembling hundreds of varieties of raw materials, including land. The developer has neither control on pricing nor can influence the supply of raw materials. The skyrocketing costs of raw materials coupled with elastic supply, have thrown the project calculations out of the window, forcing the developer to re-draw the strategies mid-way through the project. The unavoidable subsequent tweaking and rationalization leave a bad taste in every stakeholder's mouth. Damned if you do. Doomed if you don't.

LEGAL HASSLES

As the industry went into overdrive, so did the legal obligations and complications. A fair amount of developer's time is spent on legal matters adding costs, delays and uncertainties in projects. It has become part and parcel of this tricky business. Avoidable? Na!

DISRUPTIVE INCIDENTS

What was intended to be path-breaking measures, turned out to be back-breaking accidents for the real estate industry. Demonetization,

GST and, to some extent, RERA have put the real estate industry on a ventilator. The ripple effect of the chaos and disruptions that followed have put the industry on edge.

DEMAND

All the above, combined, added to the cost of production. Cost of funds and non-availability of funds was a 'Double Whammy'. With no one willing to share the burden of these steep hikes in costs, the developer was left with no option but to add a portion of these costs to the selling price. Market forces promptly came into play, causing a slump in demand. The developer felt like Abhimanyu of Mahabharat. He knew to enter Chakravyuh but didn't know to come out.

SUPPLY

As the new players, big in size and deep in pockets entered the market with more significant projects, the supply outstripped the demand. As the sales dried up, developers continued to borrow at high rates to keep the construction going. Supply continued unabated while demand dragged its feet, leaving the developer saddled with inventory that will barely cover his debts and obligations, leave alone profits. Even as the industry was about to come to terms, a death blow struck the industry, in the form of COVID, resulting in lockdown.

CANDID (COVID) REFLECTION

The lockdown has brought the whole country to a standstill. But for the real estate industry which has been silently suffering from apathy and lack of empathy, the lockdown has come as not just a 'Double Whammy' but as a bolt from the blue. An industry which is directly responsible for the survival of 275 ancillary industries, an industry which is second largest employment generator in the country, an industry that contributes almost 15% to GDP, an industry that caters to one of the most basic needs of human beings, certainly needs sympathetic view and support from every stakeholder to help it come out of the present crisis.

Having said that, one needs to bear this in mind. *"Cure Cannot Be Worse Than The Disease."*

Why is the industry suffering so much? Why does it remain silent instead of demanding prices that are fair and just? This is happening because we, as an industry, are FRAGMENTED! Awake, arise, unite and fight the injustice! Ask for the prices that the industry deserves for its efforts and value! Remain united for at least three months after the lockdown opens, and things will fall in place. Time to make yourself heard strongly in the corridors of power!

An Initiative by Central Mumbai Developers Welfare Association, CMDWA is an Association of South-Central Mumbai Developers formed to focus on 33(7) MHADA Cess Redevelopment schemes under DCPR 2034 especially Leasehold lands belonging to the Estate Department of MCGM. The association with this distinctive focus has made various representations to MCGM, has filed revenue related petitions, especially in the matter of unjust levy of LUC, Development Charges and Estate Premiums. CMDWA has also made various representations in the subject of GST and is actively pursuing the case through the judiciary. In all, as President CMDWA, Dharmesh Chheda, Owner of PrinceCare Realty, says "The prime purpose of CMDWA is to ensure that its members can undertake viable profitable and ethical business."

CHAPTER 3

REAL ESTATE'S REVIVAL IS ECONOMY'S SURVIVAL

Renowned American economist Dr. Christopher Thornberg famously said: "Economy Is Real Estate Driven, From Top To Bottom." He isn't wrong. He indicates that if the Real Estate industry is not in shape, it will drive down the economy, from top to bottom. CRASH. And the reasons are many and plenty.

PERSPECTIVE

No matter what the enthusiasts and optimists say, the Indian economy has been sliding down the slope ever since the Real Estate was put on a ventilator due to back to back policies such as Demonetization, GST, and RERA. For those who find this difficult to comprehend, let me take you down the road less travelled and least acknowledged.

Real estate provides one of the three basic necessities of human life, Makaan. The ongoing lockdown and migrant workers humanitarian crisis has only magnified the importance of this basic need more than ever. The other two necessities of human life, Roti and Kapda, are incomplete without Makaan. Be it an unbranded 'Roti' or an unbranded 'Kapda'; the real estate space is always a necessity. Be it a gala, shop, mall or large office; every commercial activity needs Real Estate. Be it a Chawl, Flat or Bungalow; every human being needs a house. From bhiga to acre to square feet, Real Estate occupies an inseparable aspect of human life.

CONTRIBUTOR

It is an undisputed fact that Real Estate is the 4th highest contributor to GDP at 15%. Add another 10% from more than 275 plus ancillary industries who are solely dependent on Real Estate industry, from nut & bolt to steel & cement, from brick & mortar to elevators & gensets, from paint to putty, indirectly contributing 25% to GDP. Real estate is the 2nd highest contributor to GDP, both direct and indirect contributions combined. Isn't this enough for recognition?

This reminds me of the famous middle-order batsman, The Wall, Rahul Dravid, who would come to bat after the top order collapsed. He takes you home safe, but the credit goes to someone who scored more than him.

PROVIDER

Sadly, the least acknowledged fact is that the Real Estate industry is 2nd largest employer in the country, directly employing more than 90% of the unskilled population and more than 70% semi-skilled population. Add to this, the employment generated by 275 plus ancillary MSME industries dependent on Real Estate sector and you have India's largest employer, still struggling for recognition. If this is not step-motherly treatment, then what is

REVITALISER

A healthy and robust Real Estate is a revitalizer for so many other industries. Imagine the number of goods required after taking possession of an empty flat or office. From White Goods to Furniture, from Electricals to Electronics, from Interiors to Exteriors, from Utensils to Automobiles, hundreds of sectors of the economy will get a boost. This is the ONLY industry which directly and indirectly contributes to so many other industries. A booming Real Estate is the best tonic for a healthy economy.

CREATOR

Real estate is all about asset creation, value enhancement, wealth creation and development. Real estate creates non-perishable assets.

Real estate creates Equity and Pride. Real estate creates landmarks and destinations. Yes, Real Estate creates ECONOMY.

ATTRACTOR

Devoid of glamour and yet attracts investors from domestic and international markets. Real estate has been one of the most prominent destinations for Foreign Direct Investment (FDI) in recent years, bringing in valuable foreign currency into the country. While many other industries are setting up base abroad, the Real Estate industry has been wooing foreign players to come to our country and set shop here. Can we be more patriotic?

BANKER

It wouldn't be wrong to call Real Estate as Bank's Banker. Because Banks bank on the collateral from Real Estate whenever they lend money to their customers. Be it home loan, education loan or construction loan; the collateral is always Real Estate asset. And Real Estate collateral is risk-free and most bankable security for their lending. Besides, the banks raise money on the Real Estate assets mortgaged with them. So, why not call Real Estate sector Bank's Banker or Banker's Bank? Either way, it makes sense.

GENERATOR

From Panchayat to Nagar Parishad, from Municipal Council to Municipal Corporation, from State Government to Central Government, Real Estate is the single revenue source with maximum varieties of taxations. GST, stamp duty, registration charges, property taxes, plan approval charges, TDR charges, fungible FSI charges, premiums, commencement certificate charges, occupancy certificate charges, excavation royalty, fire NOC charges etc. are a significant source of revenue for the government at various levels. Even after GST is implemented, the government continues to collect these levies, taxes and charges separately from the Real Estate industry.

India has more than 50% of its population below the age of 25 years and more than 65% below 35; this demographic dividend could become a curse if India cannot employ this growing youth population!

Only Real Estate & Infrastructure has the potential to provide mass employment to all forms of the workforce - Skilled, Unskilled, Semi-Skilled, Technical, Professional and Entrepreneurs

Sadly, the apathy and lack of empathy towards this crucial sector, has dealt a big blow to the economy.

Real Estate's Revival is Economy's Survival.

O Government! Listen To My Cry!

Government is the biggest beneficiary when it comes to real estate. However, it has unfortunately adopted a double standard and a step-motherly treatment when it comes to demand for reviving Real Estate Sector

While the government expects developers to reduce real estate prices, it doesn't want to provide any policy support to facilitate the same, which is ironical. The government's share is more than 50% of the money a consumer spends on real estate.

A Prominent Politician at a recently held webinar remarked: "We are trying for there to be a concession in the Ready Reckoner, but even if it's not there, you will have to Sell." The stark reality is that under Section 43 C (A) of the Income Tax Act 1961, if stamp duty value is more than actual consideration, then the stamp duty value shall be taken as the full value of consideration for computing business profits, meaning both buyer and developer will have to pay 30% of the difference in the selling price and the circle rate.

Furthermore, Ready Reckoner rates significantly influence the various charges, taxes, duty, and cess levied by the government, which is the prime reason for the Unaffordable Prices of Real Estate. Let us understand how the Government mints from Real Estate using an example of a typical real estate project in Mumbai City:

1. Stamp Duty - on buying land / taking Development Rights about 5% of RR rates

2. GST on Permanent Alternate Accommodation Agreement (PAAA) of Rehab ~ 5%

3. GST on construction materials about 5% to 28%

4. Premiums account more than 20% of the project cost
   - FSI like Fungible FSI, TDR, Incentive FSI Premium etc.
   - Expenses for Annexure A like Open Space Deficiency, Staircase Lift Premium
   - Development Cess about Rs. 5,000 per sq.m. of Plot Size
   - Development Charges about 1% on land and 4% on BUA of RR

- LUC or Land Under Construction Tax
- CFO Capitation Fee about Rs. 50 per sq.m. of Construction Area
- Labour Welfare Cess about 1% of RR of BUA
- IOD Deposit and Debris Deposit
- EWC / SC of about Rs. 580 per sq. ft. on Plot Area
- Expenses for Annexure B like DP, City Survey, MHADA, Estate etc.

5. Stamp Duty paid on Registration of Real Estate Purchase about 5%
6. GST from Home Buyers on Registering Under Construction Flats about 5% (Government classifies 45 lakhs as a benchmark for Affordable Housing which is impossible to achieve in Mumbai City especially given the charges levied by the government as mentioned above)
7. GST on Interior Work and Installations about 5% to 28%

Conclusion : Every 100 Rs. Home Buyer Spends, Government's Share is more than 50%

PROPOSED SOLUTION TO REVIVE REAL ESTATE HENCE REVIVE ECONOMY :

- One Time Restructuring
- Additional Institutional Funding
- Waiver of Penal Interest
- Policy Innovations for Triggering Demand
- Customer-Centric Tax Treatment of Real Estate
- Control of Cartelisation of Raw Material for Construction

- Home Loan at 5% interest
- Applicability of GST and its Input Tax Credit (ITC) on Real Estate
- Quick Operationalization of SWAMIH Fund

CHAPTER 4

PROPERTY PRICE CRASH – A MIRAGE!

"Real Estate prices may crash up to 20%", Screamed Economic Times quoting Mr. Deepak Parekh, Chairman of HDFC.

"Sell unsold units at No Profit No Loss Basis", Howled Business Standard attributing the quote to Mr. Nitin Gadkari, Senior Minister of the central government.

"Reduce prices and sell the inventory", Wailed CNBC TV, making Mr. Uday Kotak, banker and CII president, responsible for this quote.

"Cut prices and clear unsold stock.", Yelled The Hindu, keeping the gun on the shoulders of Mr. Piyush Goyal, Senior Minister of the central government.

The common factor between these four gentlemen is that none of them are from the Real Estate industry. Some advised the developers to simply reduce the prices; the others urged them to almost convert their business into an NGO, albeit temporarily. It's a classic example of Blacksmith advising Goldsmith, or vice versa, how to run business. We have heard about Real Estate Price Correction for last ten years. To the utter dismay of people who were genuinely in need of a home, the wait for correction ended up in them buying a home at double the price.

For the benefit of the common man, let me lay bare open a few important elements that determine Real Estate's pricing. Real Estate Market is entirely different from the Stock Market and the Gold Market. A Scrip on Stock Market can skyrocket without any fundamentals, and scrip with best credentials can crash at the sneeze of top management. Similarly, even a faint rumour of war can send Gold prices to sky-high. However, Real Estate Prices are driven by input costs. Let me disentangle this one for you.

Every project in Real Estate is an assembling unit and not a manufacturing factory. Further, each project is different from the other. And therefore, a Real Estate project is made up of as many as 250 to 300 types of materials. From a small nail to a giant elevator, from a small switch to a massive STP, everything is assembled on a piece of land, which itself is the most important and costliest material.

Let's navigate through the haze and maze of Real Estate Pricing.

LAND COST

This is the most essential component of the Real Estate industry. Sadly, as a customer, you focus only on what is built on it for you. Let me remind you, the developer doesn't determine the land price. Did you know that the land cost constitutes 40% to 60% of the total project cost? Demonetization was expected to cool down the landowner's expectations. Unfortunately, neither it has affected the appetite of the landowner, nor it has impacted the Ready Reckoner Rates of the government.

LABOUR COST

Generally, a customer doesn't realize that labour is 2nd most crucial element in the Real Estate industry. The recent spotlight on migrant workers has undoubtedly highlighted the importance of labour in the construction industry. But did you know that labour constitutes as much as 35% of the total construction cost? And post COVID-19 the cost of labour has gone up by 100% due to acute shortage. The impact will be massive.

MATERIAL COST

Cement prices have gone up by 50%. Steel prices have gone up by 25%. Prices of every other material have gone up by 20% to 30%

due to a shortage of supply and increased transportation cost. All this has happened in the last two months.

Yes. All that goes up comes down, except prices.

This will directly affect the under-construction projects. The developer will have no option but to include the additional cost to the selling price.

FINANCE COST

The cost of funds in Real Estate has been 'make or break' factor in recent years. It has attained the status of a significant cost centre. Cost of funds range from affordable 12% p.a. to astronomical 36% p.a. which is ultimately added to the selling price.

In the case of ready possession projects, the exorbitant cost of funds is already incurred. Price reduction will result in a significant loss, and the loans will turn NPA, compounding the problems for all stakeholders, including the buyers in the project.

APPROVAL COST

Also known as Statutory cost. You will be surprised to know that there is a tax beginning with almost every alphabet in English. And this cost is the heaviest on the developer. The less said, the better.

A stock market analyst is never tired of telling you to buy the stock even when the market is at its historic high. But for the same analyst, a developer's price 'was' always high, 'is' always high and 'will' always be high—a specimen of double standards.

WILL PRICES OF REAL ESTATE COME DOWN POST COVID-19?

- Last four years prices have remained stable, but the cost has increased
- Lockdown has resulted in Zero Productivity, but cost like tenants rent, the interest cost, corporate overheads etc. are still on which has further increased cost

- Recently Cement, Steel etc. announced price hikes which will add to cost

New Launches / Acquisitions - Won't happen for next 12-15 months (supply will not increase) however new demand for real estate is generated in this lockdown as people have realized the importance of owning a house. At the same time, rising costs with stable sales prices have resulted in a single-digit margin for Developers in most case.

The developer has already brought his margin down, its time the other stakeholders did too. I Don't see anyone doing that as yet, even the recent RBI package on three months moratorium was a mere deferral and not a waiver of any sort .... So as usual, Prices won't come down

Buyers Decide, whether you want to sit on the fence and burn money on overvalued gold or speculate on stocks which is extremely volatile. Real Estate is Rock Solid, at most attractive valuations of a lifetime and most importantly, it's REAL! Not just a piece of paper. I opine that Consumers should take advantage of the present Lockdown Discounts & soon to be made Monsoon Offers, Don't be surprised if Real Estate prices go back to Pre-COVID Range around Diwali 2020 !!

To conclude, the Real Estate price is arrived at, after taking into account all the costs. Gone are the days of super-profits. This is a highly competitive and price-sensitive market.

Established brands who always charge more, will have to re-visit their prices. For the rest, the stagnant prices for the last four years, have already done the needful.

For Developer - Market Is Good If The Marketing Is Good.

For Customer - Real Estate Is Not Only About Price. But Also About Value.

With Ever-Increasing Costs, *Property Price Crash Will Ever Remain As A Mirage In The Desert*

CHAPTER 5

PERILS OF PRICE CUT

Panacea Worse Than Malady

As shouts for Price Cut - from '20 % Reduction' to sell on 'No Profit No Loss Basis' - grew shriller, a pall of gloom descended on the industry. The loudest calls came from the tallest figures of India, and the media did the rest.

Some 'Lobonomics' before the serious topic.

"Price Is Sensitive. Not Humans."

"Price Elastic. Pockets inelastic."

"Let Market Forces Decide Price Before Market Forces You To Decide."

And, "The Most Selling Product Has No Price. FREE."

We have an extraordinary situation where we see a sudden spurt in raw material prices - e.g. cement prices by 30% - pushing the construction cost steeply upwards. At the same time salary of Home Buyer crashed by up to 50%. Even the famed economist Sir Robert Giffen would have struggled to explain this phenomenon!

Call it a fad; Price Cut is the most suggested remedy by experts during the slow down. But it is 'Poor Economics' and certainly not 'Sanjeevani' for all ailments. It has perils, pitfalls and consequences for all.

EXISTING CUSTOMER

The customer who bought prior to Price Cut will live with the embarrassment of being a foolish neighbour to someone who bought after Price Cut. And bitterness will last for life.

Existing customer's 'Loan To Value Ratio' (LTV) will fall, and the Home Loan Lender will ask for additional margin money or pre-pay a part of the loan. This will compound the woes of customer who is already smarting from a salary cut.

The existing customer would have already paid higher stamp duty, GST, and other statutory levies on the higher price. Because the existing customer bought earlier, he would have paid Pre-EMI interest to Home Loan Lender which is in addition to the higher price. The existing customer will be hurt to see the new customer who buys at an Advanced Stage of construction at Lesser Price while he bought at Higher Price when the project was at its Nascent Stage. Worst, if the customer cancels the transaction, his long journey for a refund will begin, given the builder's financial condition. The loss of interest paid to Home Loan Lender, Stamp duty Charges and lengthy documentation will be like salt on his wounds. Ethically, Price Cut will be grave economic injustice to the existing customer, causing him pain and anguish.

NEW CUSTOMER

Proponents of Price Cut will not know that the pleasure of owning a home at a lower price, comes at a cost. Builder is going through the ordeal of a series of shocks which has already put his business in distress. He is left with no choice but to re-work on the specifications of amenities, especially inside the homes. Builder is within his rights to do so. New customer's joy of paying the lower price will be short-lived and will be overtaken by regret and embarrassment.

Builder will resort to PLC (preferred location cost) pricing and offer the less preferred location homes at a lower price and better location homes at regular price. After all, the survival of the builder is as important as the completion of the project.

Lower price will be a stumbling block while re-selling in the future. Customer may not get better re-sale price as the prospective buyer will know his lower purchase price and accordingly make a lower offer. Even if he gets a better price, he will pay higher capital gains tax on the higher profits due to lower purchase price.

BUILDER

Demonetization, GST, RERA and now Price Cut? It will be like switching off the ventilator when the patient was still breathing. The pandemic has left a devastating impact on the builder dependent on the supply of 270 plus types of raw materials from as many sources. Suppliers have already started hiking the prices, to make up for the losses incurred during the lockdown.

Migrant labours will not return soon and labour cost, which constitutes a significant component of the project, has already shot up. Business is standstill, but the interest meter is ticking like a time bomb. Cash flow has stopped, but overheads continue. A Price Cut at this stage will be the final blow to the already bleeding builder who might sell fast at a lower price but will not be able to complete the project due to insufficient cash flow. The customer will end up buying a home that was never to be ready for occupation.

Price cut will open the floodgates of cancellations by the Home Buyers who booked at higher prices. There will be pressure on the builder for refunds, and this will result in complete breakdown. Neither the customer will get his money soon, nor the project will complete in time. Price Cut in a ready project is suicidal as the builder has incurred all the costs and sold the stock. He needs to keep his existing customers happy to avoid cancellations and protect goodwill. At the same time, he has to sell the remaining stock to cover all the costs incurred, including interest costs and principal repayment.

BANKS

Price Cut will result in a smaller book size of Home Loan Lenders, which will affect their ability to raise funds. It will result in noncompliance of LTV norms for the home loans given for homes bought at higher prices. It will also reduce the cover of collateral for the construction finance availed by the builder. Surprisingly the Price Cut calls are coming from the banking sector despite knowing the pitfalls for them.

GOVERNMENT

Price Cut will result in lower stamp duty collection, which will hurt the state exchequer, which in turn will impact the economy. The state will promptly revise upwards the rate of Stamp to make up for the loss. It will also result in lower GST collection, and the government will increase the rate of GST.

Therefore, in these circumstances, Price Cut prescribed as Panacea Is Worse Than Malady.

In other words, Cure Is Worse Than The Disease.

CHAPTER 6

(UN)AFFORDABLE HOUSING!

> '**Nothing is expensive. It's all about affordability.**'
>
> '**Affordability is not only about money. It is also about the readiness of mind to acquire.**'

Until recent, Affordable Housing was treated like Amol Palekar, the yesteryear actor of Bollywood. The demand, importance, utility, and capability was unquestionable but the glamour, stardom, glitz was either not accorded to or missing. Cut to the year 2020; Affordable Housing has a new brand ambassador in Bollywood. Nawazuddin Siddiqui. But unlike Amol Palekar's era, Nawazuddin is not only the toast of Tinsel Town but also the darling of media. Naturally, glamour and glitz follow him everywhere.

A few years ago, Affordable Housing was the second class citizen, neither attracting big realty brands nor the government's attention. But in the last couple of years, the big boys of Real Estate industry have taken a keen interest as a part of their business strategy, giving the much-required recognition to the 'poor country cousin' of realty space. Obviously, it caught the attention of the government too. Soon it found it's way into election manifesto of many political parties. From 5 Star Hotel conferences to corridors of power, none could afford to ignore 'Nawazuddin Siddiqui' of Real Estate Industry.

Within Affordable Housing, there is LIG, MIG and HIG, depending on the demographic dynamics. This indicates the mammoth size and expanse of the market. With a 1.3 billion population, and still growing fast, the Affordable Housing is the FMCG of the Real Estate industry.

The glamorous Affordable Housing has not only suitors from within the industry but also from other sectors of the economy. No wonder, the product has been evolving constantly and consistently. From an ordinary G+2 structure to skyscrapers, from a dingy one-room tenement to multi BHK apartments, from 'room to road' concept to lifestyle townships, the product has attained stardom of unimaginable proportions. In fact, there are affordable housing townships having amenities that can put to shame some of the most famous addresses in the upmarket.

While the segment name has continued to retain its 'Affordable' adjective, the home buyers' cost hasn't been reflective of it. I'm sure Bollywood producers are experiencing the same with the counterpart of Affordable Housing in Bollywood.

HOW TRULY AFFORDABLE IS AFFORDABLE HOUSING?

Ever since the unwelcomed arrival of Covid-19, the cost of steel, cement, ready mix concrete and sand, have gone up by 30%-50%. The labour-intensive Real Estate industry has had a double whammy, ever since the deadly virus invaded the human lung space. The cost of labour has gone up by almost 100% in the last 12 months. The consistently increasing transportation cost due to ever-increasing fuel prices has pushed up every other raw material cost by at least 10%-20%. The quest to match, if not out-do the competition brick by brick and amenity by amenity, has only added to the final cost of production of the supposedly Affordable Housing.

HOW PROFITABLE IS AFFORDABLE HOUSING?

Unlike luxury housing, one of the biggest eaters of profit in this sector is the fixed cost. Affordable Housing is a volume game. Due to its sheer operation size, the fixed overheads are far higher than a standalone luxury building having similar total revenue.

While a standalone luxury building will have fewer men and machinery employed, the Affordable Housing operations team is like a coalition government's jumbo cabinet. Therefore, the variable cost is also significantly higher than its luxury counterpart. Disproportionately high fixed cost and high variable cost is the biggest dampener for the Affordable Housing, making it least profitable.

IS IT (UN)AFFORDABLE HOUSING?

The limitations and constraints mentioned in the above paragraphs have forced the developers to come up with their own version of Affordable Housing. If you read the first two lines of this chapter once again, you will find that the developers have found the way to get around the minds of prospective customers by promptly and aptly modifying the very definition of Affordable Housing.

If the PRICE of an Affordable House prompts a prospective customer's mind to acquire it, the size of that house might completely mismatch his aspirations. Similarly, if the SIZE of an Affordable House prompts prospective customers' minds to acquire it, the price may not suit his pocket at all. The industry tells the customer that 'you can't have your cake and eat it too'. If the PRICE is affordable, the SIZE isn't and vice a versa.

This leads my thoughts to the dreaded question. Is Affordable Housing sustainable?

The very cyclical nature of Real Estate business calls for caution. The government policy decisions or lack of them makes it very vulnerable to frequent implosions. The skyrocketing raw material prices further fuelled by incredible fuel prices, makes this segment a 'cliff-hanger'. The 'shock and awe' economic events caused by the government's sudden announcements leave the industry in a mess. The pandemic of COVID-19 has brought with it untold misery to the developer and customer.

The ultimate result is the thinning of 'wafer-thin' margins of Affordable Housing sector. From the outside, it looks as beautiful as 'Lays' packet. But, the 'wafers' inside, know it all!

Stakeholders of this all-important segment of Real Estate can 'ill-afford' a collapse that will affect the country's socio-economic balance. They will do well to take timely action before it's too late.

The solution is more complicated than solving Fermat's last theorem.

CHAPTER 7

REBOOT REALTY

II रीboot Rॅalty II

The ongoing cricket series between West Indies and England takes my memory back to 1984. West Indies batsman Larry Gomes was not out on 96 and had lost all his partners, except one. All, including umpires, were ready to pack up as everyone knew that the 11th batsman was severely injured and had a double fractured hand while fielding, hence unlikely to bat again. Suddenly, the increasing sound of typical British clapping draws everyone's attention towards a tall man emerging from the dressing room. Left hand in heavy plaster, covering even palm, walks to the middle and takes guard with one hand. Lo and behold! He sends the very second ball he faced to the fence. He goes on to add few runs to the total while helping Larry Gomes complete his century. All the while, batting with just one hand! Yes, only one hand!

The tall man walks out once again to take the field against England in the 2nd innings, only to rip apart famed England batting line up with sensational figures of 7/53. With just one hand! Yes, just one hand!

Ladies and gentlemen, let me have the privilege to introduce you, my most favourite cricketer, the legendary, Late Malcolm Marshal. Bruised, Battered, Broken; but comes to the middle REBOOTED.

I have always started my blogs, either with some quotes or a silly joke. When I told my college-going son the title of this blog, he quipped. 'Interesting Caption'. I asked him what is interesting about it, and he, in turn, asked me to find out the meanings of the 'Boot-out' and 'Boot- off'. This forced me to double-check the meaning of 'Reboot'. I had a sigh of relief when I found that the meaning was exactly what I had meant it to be.

Almost everything connected with automation comes with the word 'Reboot'. I knew why my son found 'Reboot Realty' Interesting. For the E-gen that he belongs to, he knew, technically the word Reboot has nothing to do with Real Estate Business. After a fair amount of convincing, he gave his assent to the caption.

Friends, today Real Estate Industry certainly looks like Great Malcolm Marshal in 1984. Bruised, Battered and Broken. Though there have been several bounce backs in the past, this time around things aren't the same. Just like the Great Malcolm Marshall, the Real Estate Industry needs to Reboot. Yes, Reboot Realty.

Let's be clear about this. A reboot is not Restart.

There are **FIVE elements** to Reboot.

RE-ORIENT

We have orientation programs, especially conducted at the beginning of the Financial/Calendar/Academic year. These programs help the participants re-focus, re-look and re-dedicate to the new mission ahead. Real Estate Industry certainly needs to Re-orient itself because the mission ahead is different from the one we had a few months ago. One of the finest examples for Re-orientation is the majestic Sun Flower. It Re-orients itself with the movement of the sun in the sky. In science, it is called Heliotropism. We call it Re-orientation. Do you know what a Sun Flower does at night in the absence of sun in the sky? I leave you with the question. The answer has a big lesson for us.

RE-INVENT

I can't give a better example than a LADY. Unlike men, a lady does her best to look different every time, different from everyone, and different all the time. Sub-consciously, she is re-inventing herself every time she stands in front of EVERY mirror that comes her way. Real Estate Industry needs to find the NEW in it. From methods to madness, the industry must present a NEW LOOK to the market.

RE-ORGANIZE

If you keenly observe a fruit vendor, you will find him always busy re-arranging his inventory to make his cart and stock more appealing. It is time the Real Estate Industry takes a leaf out of his book and Re-organize every element of the business. From Men to Machine to Money to Material, a complete overhauling is the need of the hour.

RE-ALIGN

All of us have friends for reasons, friends for seasons, and friends for occasions. Similarly, relatives and other relationships of our lives vary from time to time, geography to geography and celebrations to celebrations. In our personal lives, we have learnt the art of alignment and re-alignment according to the situation. Similarly, Real Estate Industry needs to re-align every aspect of the business, from thoughts to process to people to skills. The compatibility factor in the changed scenario will prove to be a game-changer.

RE-EVALUATE

When everything is hunky-dory, one cares a damn for strengths and weaknesses. But when the industry is bruised, battered and broken, re-evaluating or re-assessing the abilities and disabilities is paramount. After all, one cannot do everything, everywhere, in every circumstance. There are different players for Test Matches, One Day International and Twenty20 and the very few who play all three formats, fall under 'LEGEND' category.

Charles Darwin would be proud of the Real Estate Industry's effort to practice his 'Survival Of Fittest' theory through these five elements. Re-orient, Re-invent, Re-organize, Re-align, and Re-evaluate.

Better a 'Reboot' than a 'Boot-out' or 'Boot-off'.

CHAPTER 8

FORTUNE FAVOURS THE BRAVE

Monsoon, It's Raining Sops For Home Buyers

'Chappar Phadke'

'Monsoon Dhamaka'

'Lockdown Bonanza'

'Ghar Baithe Ghar Basao'

Bland but these are some of the captions thrown at our face from our mobile handsets at 'Roger Federer' like consistency. What's most intriguing is that the sender is surprisingly a BUILDER or DEVELOPER.

With COVID-19 enforcing complete lockdown on the nation and the economy, it was a deathly silence at the places where once chaos ruled. Downed shutters, closed gates, silent streets, dumb and numb transports, might have warmed the hearts of over-enthusiastic environmentalists. But indeed not of the industry, economy and entrepreneurs who are the worst sufferers due to the 'yet to be controlled' pandemic.

However, there was a conspicuous exception to the above monotony. As they say, 'when the going gets tough, the tough get going,' here comes an unlikely entrepreneur who has been playing the "CLIFF-HANGER" since the last 3-4 years.

We all know that the Real Estate industry has been sailing the choppy seas due to rapidly introduced policy changes that took away breath from the industry which was already on a ventilator. The onslaught of COVID-19 would have certainly made many believe that builders and developers would soon be joining the extinct species. But that was not to be. If I say, 'just like the raw materials they use for construction, builders are made of nerves of STEEL', I'm sure I will be pardoned for the exaggeration.

The undying spirit of builders coaxes me to dig into my past blogs and bring alive the example of SUNFLOWER that never looks down even after the sun moves to the other side of the planet earth. This spirit has been on HD mode of display in Real Estate Industry, ever since the villain, COVID-19 stepped on the Indian soil. The result is, for Home Buyers this time around the twin festivals Dussehra-Diwali have arrived quite early.

GOVT. LARGESSE

Though the last one to join the party, the credit for laying the icing on the cake goes to Government Of Maharashtra, which announced a significant reduction in Stamp Duty charges and declared timeline for its restoration to the original rates in advance. This has woken up even the laziest of house hunter to make the most of this 'French Window' opened by the Chief Minister, also known as Common Man's CM. Thank you Honourable Mr. Chief Minister.

Ripple effect has been felt across the country as more CEOs of other State Governments join the 'Band Baaja Baraat,' though the Band Master is yet to reciprocate (Pun intended).

LION HEARTED BUILDER

It all began with subtle yet significant price variations introduced in the form of differential pricing, a strategy that worked well for ready possession inventory.

The under-construction projects followed suit and went a step further by introducing 'Step Up Floor Rise' pricing, a strategy that gives the same price-band up to a particular number of floors.

Some marketing savvy developers introduced assured gifts that the prospective customer couldn't buy due to the pandemic's effects. This 'instant win' ensured an instant 'Madhuri Smile' on the face of the Lady of the house, while the family came out of the salesroom of the developer after booking the Flat. Trust me the feeling is no less than the Bowler who would have clean bowled 'The Wall', Rahul Dravid.

'Pay Nothing Till Possession',

'Live Now, Pay Later',

'Ab Ghar Kharidne Keliye Sirf Ek Rupya Hi Kaafi Hai',

'Choose Your Neighbours'

The list of innovative schemes from the developers goes on and never seem to end.

For once, the developers have put to shame the MNCs vis-a-vis marketing strategies. While some developers played 'Santa' to the prospective Home Buyers, the others applied balm to distraught and exasperated victims of the effect of COVID-19 by absorbing various charges. The result was the same. Prospects turned Buyers.

The sales registers started filling sooner than expected, so much so that a courageous developer friend of mine even did Bhoomi Pujan and launched a project during the peak of lockdown. Fortune favours the brave. Well done brother. Keep it up.

Presently, a healthy marketing competition is going on in the Real Estate Industry. But in this competition 'Loser Is None & Winner is Home Buyer.' The confirmed number of bookings in its most authentic form suggests that lockdown has been a blessing in disguise for many developers and Home Buyers alike. The Home Buyer's expectation of a 'COVID19 Offer Without Infection' now meets the developer's need for a cure to 'Avoid Getting Admitted To a COVID Hospital'.

In this battle of survival, though a sure shot 'VACCINE' is not available yet, Builders and Home Buyers ensure that both survive in this pandemic while helping each other fulfil their heart's desires.

The famous Bollywood song from 'Hera Pheri' rings aloud in my ears.

'Denewala jab bhi deta, Deta Chappar Phadke'

Did I hear someone offering 100% Loan?

It's Raining Boon and Bonanza For Home Buyer. It's Monsoon.

CHAPTER 9
MARKET IS GOOD IF MARKETING IS GOOD

Proverb No.1

'There Is a Recession In The Market'

Proverb No.2

'There's No Money In The Market'

Proverb No.3

'Market Kharaab Hai'

These are some of the most common dialogues we have been hearing, which are on the cusp of becoming 'Proverbs.' If not kept under check, they might even penetrate the most vulnerable school textbooks.

My answer to all '3 Proverbs'.

'Recession Is In The Mind. Not In The Market'

'Money Is Not In The Market. It Is In The Pocket'

'Market Kharaab Nahin. Marketing Kharaab Hai'

For an Economist, a recession is a situation wherein people recall his existence. No offence to highly qualified yet unrecognized and barely qualified but thrust on us as economics pundits. For a Businessman, a recession is the absence of sale and collection. For them, the entire economic situation is summarised in the above '3 Proverbs.' For Students, starting from high school to Post Graduates, a recession is a subject consisting of complex definitions, intricate diagrams, endless tables and volumes of text that they might never use again in their life. For me, a Marketeer, a recession is a situation, resulting from the reluctance of customer, who has decided not to spend his money now, and Marketing is an 'ART' of convincing such a reluctant customer to spend his money now.

If 'Recession' is the malady, 'Marketing' is the panacea.

And therefore, *'Market Is Good If Marketing Is Good.'*

A good marketeer thrives in worst market conditions. A good marketeer never misses his focus on reluctant customer's mind and pocket. His only aim is to re-ignite the passion for his product in the customer's heart and to do so; he keeps on re-inventing himself. Therefore, the very nature of Marketing is fluid and dynamic. Marketing is like Belly Dance. The basic structure remains still and firm while the body parts move according to the music. Fundamentals of Marketing remain the same. However, the components of Marketing will keep adapting to the changes in the preferences of the customer.

This brings us to the famous 5 Ps of Marketing. Product, Price, Promotion, Place, and People. Most Marketing manuals explain these 5 Ps in an ideal market situation. The textbook on marketing management is as glamorous as a celebrity in front of a camera, but the reality might be completely different. Now let us face reality.

We are in the midst of those '3 Proverbs'. There's no customer in sight for miles. Therefore, obviously, no money in the cash box. And we all know that ONLY & ONLY a CUSTOMER can bring in the money. And ONLY & ONLY GOOD MARKETING can bring back the customer even on 'Bad Days'.

As I said earlier, the fundamentals of marketing remain the same. However, re-visiting the 5 Ps of Marketing is essential to re-ignite the passion in the heart of the customer.

PRODUCT

Just like a young lady who uses every trick to attract a handsome man or vice versa, a product too uses all the tricks to catch the attention of the 'acting too pricey' customer. The basic specifications of the product do not change. The difference is the same as that of a boy or girl's appearance on a 'normal day' and a 'date day'. Passion re-ignited. Couldn't have made it simpler.

PRICE

Good days, good price; Bad days, not a bad price, but bad 'pricing' can make way for 'worse days'. To re-ignite the passion in the hearts of the 'acting too pricey' customer, the product's price should act as a mini skirt. Long enough to cover the costs and short enough to arouse customer's interest. Sorry if I sound naughty.

PROMOTION

Many marketers create commotion instead of promotion during bad days, and others go silent as if they are mourning. Bad days call for smart promotions. Marketing books do not tell you about Carpet Bombing, Cluster Bombing, Surgical Strike, Bouquet Marketing etc. Well, wooing an 'acting too pricey' lady, needs a lot of creativity. Scratch your brain—best of luck.

PLACE

Who would want to take his lady love on a date to a stinky place? Spruce up. Deck up. Clean up. Let the fragrance reach the doors of 'acting too pricey' customer.

PEOPLE

I must tell you, no matter how well you re-visit the other 4 Ps, employees can bring everything to nought. An ill-trained, demotivated and unsettled workforce is the most significant liability on the balance sheet. And they can prolong 'Market Kharaab Hai' days.

In 1989, I saw a signboard in Johnson & Johnson which read, 'Employees Are Our Best Available Resources'. Mind you, during bad days, from 'Watchman' to 'Chairman', everyone is a 'Salesman'.

Same 5 Ps but differently treated. No definitions. No diagrams. No tables. No formulas. Simply 'Good Marketing' and 3 Proverbs will turn out to be 3 Myths.

CHAPTER 10

ALL IS WELL WHEN YOU SELL

In the famous Bollywood blockbuster 3 IDIOTS, whenever there's a crisis, the hero would prompt everyone to say "All is well". He even uses it to revive an almost dead new-born baby. Very inspirational!

Well, for the real estate industry, circumstances are not entirely different. The industry is on a ventilator. Can we simply keep saying "All is well" and wait for that miracle customer walk through the door, with money in hand to bail us out?

In my 23 years of Sales & Marketing action involving 50000+ units in real estate space, the sentence from developers I heard most is "market is bad". And I have always countered it with "market is good if marketing is good". Perhaps, the other way to put it in filmy style is All is WELL when you SELL.

If we observe keenly, we find that 'Most Leveraged' businesses tie-up with 'Worst Lender' and 'Least Leveraged' businesses tie-up with 'CUSTOMER'. Unfortunately, the real estate industry has engrossed itself in planning, liaisoning, approvals and construction, so much so that it has never bothered to tie up with the CUSTOMER. For most developers, advertising is marketing with 'cost per lead' centred digital campaign, lowest rent based billboards, poorly designed leaflet distribution etc. Worst, the executing agency would have never even visited the construction site but entrusted with the responsibility to promote the product.

In one of my blog titled "Turn Around Of Real Estate. Courtesy Covid-19", I have projected the industry's turnaround based on favourable external factors. But for the turnaround of an individual developer experiencing a recession, which is essentially the absence of sales, the internal factors within his organization need to be revamped to suit the new world that we will enter post lockdown.

So how do we approach sales & marketing of our real estate, post lockdown?

First and foremost, revamp, refurbish, renovate, reinvigorate, rejuvenate your sales and marketing team who would have hit the lowest ebb by now. A demoralized team is the most significant liability on your balance sheet. Remember, this is the team which will get you interest-free money from the market.

Secondly, outsource critical activities, including but not limited to, sole selling & marketing, to experienced professionals. These professionals have not only seen but worked through multiple cycles of recessions. They have few tricks up their sleeves to kick start your sales post lockdown.

Finally, sales & marketing is the most important activity and therefore, do earmark a decent budget that is recovered almost immediately. We need to change our '2% cost' approach towards sales and marketing. Legendary Jack Welch once said: "Change before you have to."

ALL IS WELL when you SELL. Happy SELLING.

CHAPTER 11

LENDERS COULD MAKE 'HOUSING FOR ALL' POSSIBLE

HOME LOAN LENDERS Must Rescue Home Buyer & Now.

"Indians should work for 60 hours a week for the next 2-3 years to revive the economy"- Narayan Murthy.

"Up to 50% of salary will be cut"- Mukesh Ambani.

The thundering bolts from the towering figures of Indian Industry remind me of a historic day, 24th November 1981, when devastating fast bowlers of all time - Andy Roberts, Michael Holding, Joel Garner, Malcolm Marshal and Collin Croft - took field together. They must have sent chills down the spines of even spectators!!

The most respected professional in the country, advocates for extra hours of efforts by employees and the richest man in India, announced pay cuts up to 50% in his company, India's largest. The message is clear, 'Work More, For Less'. 80% of the Home Buyers are salaried, and 'Work More, For Less' diktat has dashed millions of hopes of owning a dream home.

Disregarding developers' precarious situation, all and sundry are preaching through the latest fad of webinars, about what developers need to do to help Home Buyers. This is like 'expecting a lame, help the blind cross the road at a junction without traffic signals'.

But there's someone who CAN and MUST help Home Buyers at this unprecedented critical juncture of their life. HOME LOAN LENDERS. They have an obligation to help the Indian middle class realize their dream and help the nation achieve HOUSING FOR ALL.

Take an example of a family, earning a monthly salary of Rs.1,00,000/-, before the pay cut was announced. Under the present lending norms, the family will get a loan amount of Rs.71,00,000/- for 20 years @8% p.a. interest. With this loan amount, they can buy a property of gross value worth Rs.85,00,000/-.

Under 'Work More, For Less' scenario, let's assume the family's salary is Rs.70,000/- per month, now reduced by 30%. Under the present lending norms, the family will get a loan amount of Rs.50,00,000/- for 20 years @8% p.a. interest. With this loan amount, they can buy a property of gross value worth Rs.60,00,000/- instead of Rs.85,00,000/ which was possible when salary was Rs.1,00,000/-.

Consequences are grave to all stakeholders. Firstly, the Home Buyer will have to downsize his dream to a smaller home. Secondly, as a result, the Home Loan Lender's value of assets in the books will reduce drastically. Thirdly, the developer will be saddled with an unsold inventory of larger homes. All three will suffer along with the economy. This will not help the nation.

Yes, as I said earlier, Home Loan Lenders can undoubtedly help.

ROI (RATE OF INTEREST)

Reduce interest rates to the levels of the year 2003-04, i.e. @6% p.a. which will bring down the EMI and increase the loan amount.

TENURE

Working-age has increased along with increased life expectancy. Make 30-year loan a norm with an age limit of 75 years. This will make the Home Buyer eligible for higher loan amount at a lesser rate of EMI. Majority of the loans are pre-closed anyway.

Introduce 40 years loan to encourage youngsters to buy a home early in life. Longer the tenure, lesser the EMI and higher the loan amount.

LTV (LOAN TO VALUE RATIO)

Many have exhausted their savings during the lockdown, and many have lost their savings in the stock market crash. A higher LTV will increase the loan amount and bring down the self-contribution towards purchasing a home. Make 90% LTV a norm on the home's gross value instead of prevailing 90% LTV on the agreement value.

FOIR (Fixed Obligation to Income Ratio)

Most of the middle-class families have a second income in cash to take care of day to day needs. Moreover, the Indian middle class are big savers. Increase FOIR to 70%, instead of the prevailing 60%, which will enhance the Home Buyer's loan eligibility.

See how these four initiatives by Home Loan Lenders will help the family earning a reduced monthly income of Rs.70,000/- after pay cut.

The family will get a loan amount of Rs. 81,00,000/- with reduced ROI of 6%, increased tenure of 30 years and increased FOIR of 70%. Further, with LTV of 90% on the gross value of the home, the home buyer can buy a property of gross value worth Rs.90,00,000/-. Moreover, self-contribution will also come down drastically, and his dream of owning a home of his choice is fulfilled.

If the Home Loan Lenders heed to our humble pleas, it will be all the way, a WIN-WIN-WIN situation for BUYER-LENDER-DEVELOPER and will ensure survival with minimum damage.

Survive Now. Cry Later.

STOP THE TSUNAMI OF NPAS BEFORE IT IS TOO LATE!

"The balance sheets of the Government & Consumers are not in a state to help much. Only reforms can, in our view" – HSBC India

BACKGROUND

- Global Credit Rating Agency Fitch revised India's Sovereign Rating Outlook to Negative
- Fitch downgraded rating from Stable to Negative citing Risks due to continued acceleration in the number of COVID 19 Cases as India eases Lockdown curbs
- Over the past few weeks, all 3 Global Rating Agencies have downgraded India's Rating – Standard & Poor, Moody's Investors Services & Fitch Rating
- Economic activity is expected to contract by 16% in the first half of FY21: HSBC India
- India's GDP to contract 7.2% in the ongoing financial year: HSBC India
- "India lacks a strong growth driver" Problems Mix include Reduced Consumer Spending, Labour Shortage due to Reverse Migration, Insufficient Fiscal Stimulus, Lack of Fresh Lending by Financial Institutions: HSBC India
- New Asset-Quality Challenges have Emerged due to rise in Unemployment and Salary Cuts

REASON FOR THE IMPENDING TSUNAMI OF NPAS

- HSBC expects India to see a lower growth trend after the pandemic
- India set to witness the lowest level of output since the turn of the millennium, with lower Labour Input & weaker Capital growth which is not expected to be at pre-pandemic level till FY23
- Most Businesses had ZERO Revenue during Lockdown
- WFH was not possible in most job roles

- Lockdown was a period of almost zero work productivity for most individuals
- Salary Cuts and Lay-Offs became the New Normal in Lockdown
- India's unemployment rate rises to 27.11 % in May 2020 amid COVID 19 Crisis: CMIE
- It's a 210% rise in unemployment as compared to March 2020 which stood at 8.74%
- The unemployment level was at an all-time high in Urban India at almost 30% in May 2020
- COVID Impact: 2 in every 5 employees are facing salary cuts according to an online survey by ET
- According to an Economic Times study, almost 40% of respondents are facing Salary Cuts
- Nearly 15% of the respondents are set to lose their jobs
- 18% of the employees likely to lose their jobs have work experience of 10-14 years

INDIAN BANKING SECTOR

- Bank Credit end of Feb 2020 stood at Rs. 89.8 lakh crore as per data released by RBI
- Personal Loans (Rs. 25.3 lakh crore) are almost 28% of total Bank Credit (TOI, April 2020)
- Personal Loans has outgrown credit to the large industry especially in last one year
- Home Loans accounting for 15% of bank credit (Rs. 13.30 lakh crore)
- Other Personal Loans including unsecured credit is Rs. 7 lakh crore
- Services Sector accounts for Rs. 24.3 lakh crore of bank loans (27% of bank credit)

- Service Segment is most affected in COVID 19 as it has hotels, tourism etc. part of the portfolio
- Loans to NBFCs by Banks grew by 22% in last one year to Rs. 7 lakh crore

THE "REAL" ESTATE LOAN "EXPOSURE" (SOURCE MCA & CRE MATRIX)

- Rs. 8.1 Lac Crore Active Sanctioned Loans to Indian Real Estate Sector across all Asset Classes
- MMR, NCR & Bengaluru remain exposed to around 80% of the Rs. 8.1 Lac Crore RE Loan Book
- 58% Realty Loans are by Banks, 23% by NBFC and 10% by HFCs
- 75% Realty Loan Distribution is of ticket Size more than 25 crores
- Rs. 2.4 Lac crore has the potential to get direct "much needed" relief if 1 Year OTR is provided
- Almost 81% Real Estate Loans already had Loan Repayment Start Date before March 2020

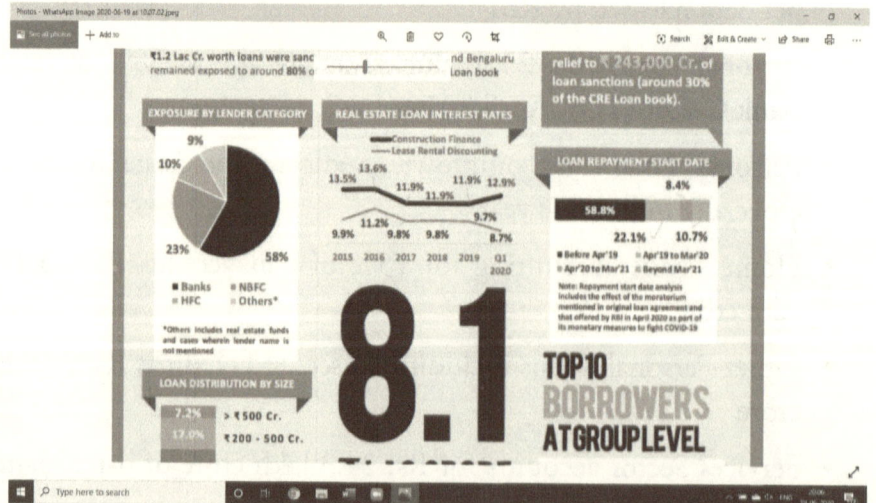

Despite the cuts in REPO Rate by RBI, Banks & NBFC have not passed the Benefit to Developers

CONCLUSION

MSME Relief in Realty is being provided for loans below 25 crores but 75% Realty Loan Distribution is of ticket Size more than 25 crores. What about Realty Loans above 25 crores?

One Time Restructuring (OTR) is the only pragmatic solution to save the economy!!

The impending Tsunami of NPAs needs to be stopped before it's too late.

IF NOT NOW, THEN WHEN ??

CHAPTER 12

SCIENCE OF HOME BUYING

It has been a fad to connect the word 'Art' to almost every activity, so much so that the word 'Art' itself has lost its 'Elite' place and meaning. From manoeuvring the ball in any sports to culinary kitchen recipes, from farcical oratory to deceitful survival in Politics, the word 'Art' is used to sanctify the activities which have no connection whatsoever, even remotely, with 'Art'. Worse, 'Real Art' has lost its place of pride to 'Commercial Art'.

In the recent past, the pronoun 'Artist' has been hijacked by politicians. The 'Art' of 'Buying & Selling' is now their exclusive domain.

'Art'. It requires a specific set of skills which are not in everyone's possession. But I feel, post COVID-19, it is set to change. 'Science' has replaced 'Art'. If selling a home has changed to science, then buying a home has changed to science too. Thanks to COVID-19, the Science of Home Buying is already changing the contours of the industry.

Now that the New Education Policy has been announced, we must request Education Department to add 'Science of Home Buying' as a unique chapter in 'Home Science' subject.😀. From the way we live to the way we let others live, COVID-19 has practically changed everything in our lives. Today, our lives are guided, guarded and goaded by almost every branch of science! How can Home Buying remain without a whiff of science?

PRODUCT @ DOOR

Once a reluctant and rude builder but now an overwhelmingly willing service provider, the developer has evolved and ensured that he provides the Home Buyer with every detail on WhatsApp, SMS, Email, Tele-call, Video Call etc. The information is shared in the form of Website links, Videos, PDF/JPEG files etc. Home Buyer has complete access to information at his fingertip.

SITE VISIT @ HOME

Gone are the days when Home Buyer had to plan a personal site visit well in advance. The Science & Technology has ensured, thanks to COVID-19, that the project is virtually brought to the door of Home Buyer through live streaming of video by the sales personnel of developers. Be it Sample Flat, Show Flat or the flat which Home Buyer intends to buy, the live video brings everything into the living room of Home Buyer. The best part, he can record and repeatedly see the video at will.

LOCALE @ FINGERTIPS

Various Apps, including Google Map, help eliminate the manual error and effort to locate the project and measure the distance from different locations. This safeguards the Home Buyer from erroneous information from the sales staff. On his palm, the Home Buyer can check the building's orientation, the direction of flats, neighbourhood, measure distance to various places etc. The Science & Technology has come to Home Buyer's aid, saving precious time, energy, money and other resources. Read 'Vastu' on your palm by instantly checking on the Compass App.

BOOK @ EASE

It is a matter of great pride that Home Buyer's enthusiasm has kept the Real Estate Industry in good stead despite lockdown. The quick adaptation to 'Science Of Home Buying' has helped the Home Buyer close the transactions with very attractive propositions put forward by the hard-pressed developers during the lockdown, thus saving huge money, effort, and time much to the joy of Home Buyer.

Credit/Debit cards, RTGS, NEFT and other online payment methods have added teeth to the 'Science Of Home Buying' by eliminating tediousness, delays and risks involved in cheque transactions.

DOCS @ WILL

The government too was quick to respond to the situation. Revolutionary steps of Online Stamp duty payment and registration at the developer's office instead of dingy sub-registrar office, are proof enough to the claim that science and Technology can indeed improve Home Buying Experience. Wait! It's not over. The government is also mulling over the idea of getting the registration done at the customer's home! Goodbye to dingy, dirty and tricky registration office. Balle Balle!!

FINANCE @ HAND

Housing Finance Companies and Banks have already started accepting documents sent through emails. Personal discussion (PD) is taking place over Zoom or Google Meet. The time taken from application for a loan to disbursement has been reduced substantially. Paperwork and numerous visits to the bank have been curtailed across all functions. The ease of availing a Home Loan has just begun.

POSSESSION & POST POSSESSION

No more visits to the builder's office to sign documents before possession. All pre-possession documents are sent through email.

Many builders have already developed unique Apps to take care of post possession services. Customer need not call or visit the builder's office. Simply upload the service required on the App and post possession team does the needful.

They say, 'For Boy & Girl, Life Changes After Marriage'.

Unlike in marriage, 'For Home Buyer & Builder, Life Has Changed For Better'. Of course, marriage between buyer & builder is a pre-condition.😊

For once, something is changing from 'ART' to 'SCIENCE'—the science of Home Buying.

CHAPTER 13

POST COVID, DEVELOPER'S PROFITS ARE IN THE KITCHEN

If there's one sector of the economy which will have to deal with the unheard Multi-Whammy, it is real estate. Using "double whammy" word would have sounded too little, for, COVID-19 pounding would leave a cavity that would take a long time to heal.

The most unfortunate part is that the long wait for revival, punctuated by the trio of Demo-GST-RERA, actually ended up with a massive tumble due to COVID-19. However, the good news is that it can't go below this. Nothing can go worse than complete halt. Now the choice between Re-Start and Re-Boot lies with the developer. Tech-savvy would know the difference between the two.

In one of my previous blog, I placed before you factors that will help turn around the industry. However, one must bear in mind that post COVID-19, the industry will never be the same again. Let's examine the changes that we will have to live with hereafter.

CONSOLIDATION

First and foremost, what the advent of RERA initiated, COVID-19 will accomplish. Corporate and big family-run developers will continue while small and medium enterprises will fall aside.

TOPLINE

Topline will taper off as there will be tremendous pressure on selling price and sales volume.

OPERATIONS

If not all, most operational aspects of real estate business have to be brought under Standard Operating Practices to sustain and survive future shocks.

COSTS

Since the customer will decide the selling price, the developer will have to focus on his KITCHEN to manage and achieve cost efficiency. Wafers will be thicker than profits in the days to come. Cook will decide the margins.

HUMAN RESOURCE

Jumbo size teams with astronomical pay packets will be a thing of the past. Partially outsourcing activities like marketing and sales, HR, finance and accounts, construction with material will directly or indirectly save time, energy, space, money and other resources.

BOTTOMLINE

Most developers will struggle to be out of the red zone. The high cost of finance will have already eaten into the future profits of the project.

Therefore, the only place the developers can look for profits is in their KITCHEN. Cook a quick meal with good but inexpensive ingredients, serve it hot to the customer, and he will pay you right price!

HAPPY COOKING

WE NEED TO LOCK DOWN THE COVID MENTALITY

As if the challenges we have been already facing aren't enough, we have one of the biggest challenges coming our way, in the days to come. COVID MENTALITY. When the lockdown was announced, we went through various emotions such as panic, fear, anxiety, worry, uncertainty, stress, doubts and many more. As the lockdown continues, the emotions have become more intense and haunt us due to the onslaught of unpleasant information that is not exactly music to our ears. As social animals, every human being under lockdown is connected with our lives in one way or another. And they too are going through the same emotions, as we are. The similarity ends here.

Now the challenging part begins. The people in our lives are from various backgrounds with different abilities and capacities to deal with emotions. It will be a lie if we say the lockdown hasn't affected us emotionally. It has affected everyone's emotions in different proportions. Clinically, if a human being goes through a particular set of emotions for a prolonged period, there are bound to be psychological, physical, physiological and behavioural changes. Imagine people with all these changes, coming into our lives once again, post lockdown with something that I dare to call COVID MENTALITY. World and people will never be the same again.

How do we deal with this problem we have never faced in the past?

There are various categories of people who form part of our business life broadly categorized as INTERNAL CUSTOMER & EXTERNAL CUSTOMER. Let us begin with the most critical internal customer. With a bottom-up approach, we have lower management staff, middle management staff, senior management staff, top management staff and the promoters. Now let us list out external customer. Buyer, supplier, contractor, labour, associate, lender, professional and partner, each of these categories have been affected differently by COVID MENTALITY.

Good news is that, unlike COVID-19, custom-designed medicine for COVID MENTALITY is available in stages for different categories, developed during this lockdown period.

ORIENTATION PROGRAM

This program helps people to move from disorientation to reorientation, helping them start anew with more focus on the work.

CONDITIONING CAMP

This program will introduce people to the concept of conditioning mind, body, soul and its importance in professional advancement.

WAR PLAN

This program will make people ready for the humungous task ahead involving catch-up with backlog and survival.

Each program is custom-designed for different categories with different work cultures. Each program's duration is 3-5 hours and conducted in a QUARANTINED atmosphere to ensure best results.

Let's LOCKDOWN THE COVID MENTALITY.

CHAPTER 14

IS REALTY STRONG ENOUGH FOR COVID-19

In 1983, when India went to England to play in the Cricket World Cup, Kapil Dev & Co had the tag of 'Minnows'. What followed is part of folklore and a great lesson for anyone who faced adversity in life. The 'David vs Goliath' final match of the 1983 World Cup between India and West Indies gives us goosebumps even today. 'Minnows' winning the World Cup by beating the 'Giants' is akin to a Corona infected patient walking out of a COVID hospital, alive.

Real estate is a cyclical business, downturn and adversity are not new to the developer fraternity. One of the most complex businesses, Real Estate, is full of intricacies, complexities and uncertainties. I always relate the Real Estate industry to the 'Chakravyuh' of Mahabharata. While Abhimanyu knew how to break into the 'Chakravyuh', he did not know how to come out of it, and he paid the price with his life.

Unprecedented and unimaginable economic policy decisions caught many Abhimanyus' (read builders) in the Chakravyuh of Real Estate. Even as the Abhimanyus' of real estate were combating these unfriendly economic enemies, here comes the enemy of the World Economy, the pandemic of COVID-19.

When the entire country was shut down on 21st March 2020, a grinding halt was more pronounced and visible in the Real Estate industry. The mass exodus of construction industry workers (almost 80% of India's unskilled workers employed in this industry), restrictions of movement of people and a complete shutdown of banking system put the whole sector in COVID hospital. But, this time, the Abhimanyus' of Real Estate were already battle-hardened with unmatched survival instincts, courtesy Demonetization, GST, RERA, etc.

An industry known for its conventional method of doing business, this time around, builders quickly adopted modern techniques to keep their sales registers busy. It is pertinent to note that poor attempts were made to boost the market sentiments by fancy imaginary sale figures published. However, as the lockdown progressed and the customers reconciled with the fact that Corona is here to stay for longer than the proverbial '21 days', the real figures of sale started gathering steam.

The curse of Corona brought with it a fair share of blessings in disguise too. On the one hand, the 'fence-sitter' buyer realized the need of owning a home more than ever. On the other hand, a 'stiff-nosed' developer loosened the fist to accommodate a very demanding customer. In came the matchmaker, the bank, to stitch a deal between a developer and the Home Buyer. What followed is nothing short of a miracle. The bookings started flowing in so much so that, many developers clocked sale figures better than pre-Corona days.

Revised prices, reduced rate of interest, EMI holidays, big-hearted freebies and, to some extent, the scare of not owning a home in situations like Corona, proved to be the significant factors that tilted the scale in favour of the industry.

Today, even as I give finishing touches to this book, the Real Estate Industry is functioning near normal. The most heartening aspect that needs to be applauded is the customers' enthusiasm. There is a definite surge in demand from those who have been staying on rent so far. Thanks to the pandemic, COVID-19. The customers seemed to have realized that it is better to be quarantined in their own home than a rented one.

With the gradual restoration of long-distance trains, the construction workers have been returning to the sites. The supply of raw materials has improved as road transport is open for movement of goods. Work-From-Home (WFH) is the new buzzword in the employment sector. Most offices are functioning virtually. The outdated patriarchy term, 'Housewife', is already a thing of past. Now we have 'House Husband' who works from the house.

Many developers have resorted to site visits by appointment, to avoid unnecessary crowding. This has also resulted in avoiding casual site visits or window shopping. Developers have installed advanced sanitizing equipment to assure the customer of his safety and well-being. Pick up and drop facility has undoubtedly helped the customer to build his confidence. It has also helped the developer to ensure that only genuine customers walk into the salesroom.

While humankind is yet to win the battle with COVID-19, the Real Estate industry seemed to have already gained the upper hand over the pandemic. Call it 'David vs Goliath' or 'West Indies vs India' in 1983 WC Final, but for now, Real Estate industry seemed to have won the battle.

Strength lies not in physique, but in resolve.

Real estate has resolved to WIN.

CHAPTER 15
NEW NORMAL: REAL ESTATE STRATEGIES POST LOCKDOWN

TURN AROUND OF REAL ESTATE. COURTESY COVID-19

The very caption might sound premature, as we are amid a nationwide lockdown. The casualty figures are as scary as the economic indicators that are dished out regularly by the experts prophesying doom ahead. For the developed world, India and China have always been the favourite 'son and daughter' who work harder than others to keep their houses running. And when everything is hunky-dory, parents tend to turn a blind eye to almost every silly mistake of favourite children, unless one of them causes a pandemic.

China's phenomenal growth is attributed to its ability to garner the lion's share of global investments in the last two decades. Every forbidden issue such as blatant plagiarisms, patent violations, poor human rights record, etc. was sacrificed on the altar of 'brute capitalism'. Well, one fine morning the developed world wakes up to see the dead bodies flying in every direction in their country, and to their dismay, they find that their favourite child has played naughty, by pulling a blanket over the deadly virus COVID-19. By then, things had already turned bad for the world and calls for retribution grew louder.

In comes India, with its ability to match China in meeting the expectations of the developed world and its vast experience in fighting epidemics of the past. The federal structure of India has never come to the fore as much it has now. Suddenly, the developed world finds a prime minister in every state of India, keeping aside political affiliations and rhetoric, rising to the occasion, fighting the deadly COVID-19, the way, only India can. India has already won the battle even before the war ends.

What does this mean to the developed world? Will the capital flow re-align? Will India be the toast of the developed world? Will COVID-19 be a blessing in disguise for India?

Undoubtedly, the pandemic's short-term impact on our 'already fragile economy' will be felt in every sector, including real estate. The Indian government was forced to swing into action. The cascading effect of the already announced stimulus package and the ones to be announced will turn around the real estate sector.

Let's see the factors that will help turn around the real estate sector post COVID-19.

TRUST

These days, the most frequent question we hear in the salesroom is "is the project RERA registered?" With RERA in place, a great deal of trust has been already restored among the customer community and the society in general.

INTEREST RATES

Banks have already started reducing interest rates on home loans, and I won't be surprised if the rates come down further to 2004-05 levels.

PRICES

With almost two months of absence of any sales, builders will be anxious and eager to catch up with the backlog to meet the cash flow requirements. It will only be wise to make the prices attractive to entice the customer.

STOCK MARKET

Blood bath on the stock market in the aftermath of COVID-19 will push the middle class away from SIPs and MFs. A sizable chunk can be expected to come to the real estate sector.

WEAK RUPEE

NRI community which was sitting on the fence so far will make the most of the triple bonanza of a depreciated rupee, reduced home loan rates and attractive prices.

PENDING DECISIONS

There will be a sudden rush of customers who postponed their decisions due to lockdown, travel restrictions, uncertainty and anxiety.

Add to this, India's increased stature in the international community's eyes because of the stellar role played in not only containing the pandemic but also helping other countries. This will make India the favourite destination for foreign investments, real estate being the direct beneficiary.

Are we ready?

STRATEGIES TO BE ADOPTED BY DEVELOPERS POST LOCKDOWN

FINANCE
- Restructure facility with extended Principal Moratorium, Interest Moratorium & Top-Up Facility
- Refinance the capital with better terms
- Revise the Cashflows and Business Plan
- Analyze your financial leverage and optimize the capital structure, we would recommend less issue of debts for the projects
- If you have not yet, start exploring other development models like Joint venture, Joint Development and Development Management (basically an asset-light model).
- Control your costs and Increase liquidity within the firm
- Adopt a slightly aggressive strategy for old collections

MARKETING
- Communicate: Real Estate Acha Hai, Real Estate Safe Hai, Real Estate He Sahi Hai
- Your Website is your Sample Flat!
- Focus heavily on Digital marketing
- Introduce Virtual Reality & Walkthroughs
- Inculcate Technology to a great extent
- Increase the use of CRM software
- Shift from Physical Campaigns to Online Campaigns

- Come up with creative and innovative benefits to the customers; prevent offering unrealistic discounts we need to be united to keep the margins healthy
- Reduce Marketing Spend till FMCG & Automobile Sales Increase
- Think of Safety & Sanitation precautions to be taken for Site Visits
- Increase use of Tele Marketing
- Price Reduction is not the solution, focus on product design and characteristics

SALES
- Interact with Channel Partners (CP) to get Pulse of Market
- Try for direct customer deals and pass them the CP incentives
- Don't encourage if CP's are being opportunistic about brokerage structures
- Incentivize Referral Customers
- Subvention Scheme is the solution to revive demand for under-construction
- Schemes like 10:90 (Builder Subvention) should be evaluated well before offering the same to customers
- Be flexible with your ask, try and bring the customer to even terms, use spot discounts instead of public announcements.
- Periodic virtual review interactions with the brokers for improved morale, feedback and action plan for improving sales efficiency
- Focus on loyalty sales as a key lever in delivering on sales revenues
- Focus on completing projects as fast as possible to ensure sales

DEALING WITH CUSTOMERS & INVESTORS

- Conduct Virtual Meetings; Communication is the Key!
- Call each customer and apprise them about the revised timelines
- Send them regular monthly work updates for first six months post lockdown
- Introduce hassle-free documentation by moving online
- Handle every complaint with 100% assistance
- Be true with them, pacify them for what's coming and offer discounts on upfront payments
- Offer Price Protection & Refundable Booking amount
- Flexible Payment Schedule

DEALING WITH EMPLOYEES, STAFF

- Communicate, Communicate and Communicate with Honesty & Transparency
- Reserve Cash Flow, Give Sustenance Pay, Avoid Job Cuts!
- Rationalize Salaries, No Increments this Year
- Treat your employees & labour as your family. Ultimately, it's their effort that will bring you out of this crisis, make them a "Part of You" - more than ever
- Halt new recruitment if not extremely necessary
- Focus on outsourcing tasks instead of in-house operations.
- Develop a sense of inclusion, lead from the front
- Make sure all your workers/employees are heard at the top level
- Ensure the health and safety of labourers and employees
- Lead and motivate them to achieve targets and offer performance-based incentives
- Increase Productivity with Technology and ERP Systems

DEALING WITH PROFESSIONALS (ARCHITECT, LAWYER, CA)

- All the consultants can be dealt using Web calls, as they have high client exposure in daily life, it will be advisable to avoid the meeting for some time
- Deal with a consultant on a need basis only
- Consult on their views and ideas of tackling the crisis.
- Take all their advice seriously and be open to innovation and change in long-used processes
- Request Consultants to accept part payment now and balance on completion of project or receipt of sales accruals

DEALING WITH VENDORS

- Assure them payment will be available, now is the time to stand by them
- DO NOT Renegotiate the existing contracts of vendors/contractors
- Communicate with them and instil trust in the clearance of dues by making prompt payment
- Mutually develop new prices and timelines
- Establish relationships and ensure both survive the crisis
- Insist on Technological Upgrades
- Safety, Security of Labours is of Paramount Importance
- Financial Security of Assurance of Receipt of Payment is of utmost importance

www.ingramcontent.com/pod-product-compliance
Lightning Source LLC
Chambersburg PA
CBHW021008180526
45163CB00005B/1936